—— A DEEPER ——
UNDERSTANDING OF
BIBLICAL
CONCEPTS

RONALD D. GORDON

© 2024. Ronald D. Gordon all rights reserved
ISBN 979-8-9903674-3-2
www.gordonpianoservice.com

CONTENTS

FOREWORD

Ron Gordon Pursuing After the Life of the Spirit

I've known Ron for approximately ten years. I lead a men's ministry, where Ron attends meetings, and I have observed that he has a hunger for the things of the spirit. As others may not have received so readily what the Scriptures clearly say about the gifts, Ron has had no doubt in his mind that this was for him. And he was not going to allow this to pass him by (meaning he wasn't going to live his life without experiencing all that God freely gives).

I believe God uses Ron primarily because of his childlike faith (posture). He has no timidity about asking anyone if he can pray for them. One of Ron's gifts is ministering to whomever he meets, whether on the streets, on college campuses, or in customers' homes where he tunes pianos.

You are about to take a journey that will make you smile regardless of whether you are a new believer or one who has been in the trenches (seasoned). You will be introduced to things in the Bible that will minister and equip you in the areas of healing, grace, salvation, and quiet time with God.

We have a way of complicating Scripture. Ron has a way of communicating the simplicity of Scripture.

Get Ready! Get Set! Go!

Paul Powers
President,
Men of Honor Ministries

ACKNOWLEDGMENTS

There are many who have helped and encouraged me in the process of writing this book. Paul Powers has been a friend, mentor, and encourager for me. I'm especially grateful to Paul for writing the foreword to this book.

I'm also grateful for my wife, Mary, who has spent many hours editing and typing the manuscript. In addition, she has done all the footwork in every category where the internet was involved. She has been my greatest fan and provided much encouragement. Without her, this book would not be in your hands.

Pastor Rick Kardell and his secretary, Wendy Lawson, are responsible for this book even being envisioned in the first place. Thank you, Pastor Rick, for your book, *We Just Want to Testify*. Pastor Rick and Wendy reached out to many for articles for his book. It's because of both of them that I began writing articles and discovered my love for writing.

I am very grateful for the many Bible teachers and friends of the past who gave me encouragement and understanding in the things of God.

Most of all, I want to thank God, my Father, and my Lord Jesus Christ, not only for the understanding I have, but that I'm still here to share this with others.

PREFACE

About a year ago I wrote some articles for a devotional book being assembled by a pastor friend of mine. Friends began to encourage me with how much they enjoyed reading these articles. They said it cleared things up for them, and I realized how needed these revelations would be for the entire Body of Christ.

I believe the Bible is the Word of God and is inherently accurate. Things that we hear and that are practiced in the Christian world often do not line up with the scope of what the Bible really teaches. I've read and researched the Bible for about fifty years. I've often found that just because something is accepted as true by the majority of people doesn't make it true; i.e., the world is not flat. We have to line things up with the Word of God to see whether they are true.

> *Sanctify them through thy truth: thy word is truth.*
> John 17:17

We also have to be willing to change our beliefs at times if we want to be set free.

And ye shall know the truth, and the truth shall make you free.

John 8:32

The purpose of this book is not to just "kill sacred cows," but to set people free in Christ.

INTRODUCTION

Thank you for picking up my book, *A Deeper Understanding of Biblical Concepts*. These articles (chapters) concern many different subjects and embrace a large variety of Biblical topics. You might disagree with one, and then be thrilled with the next one.

You are under no obligation to agree with everything I have written. From my experience, I have noted that when someone vehemently disagrees with something he reads, his tendency is to throw out the entire book. I am requesting that if you find an article that cuts across your belief system, please read on to the next one.

I've been encouraged by readers who have testified to me how they have been set free in certain areas by the insight they've gained from this book.

Each chapter is a self-contained thesis, although there are overlapping themes in some of them. You will likely find many of these articles to be a springboard for your Bible study groups. It could also be used as a devotional, but many find they finish the entire book in one or two sittings.

I hope you enjoy *A Deeper Understanding of Biblical Concepts* as much as I enjoyed putting it together. I pray it will enhance your freedom in Christ.

All Scripture, unless otherwise noted, is quoted from the King James Version (KJV).

Ronald D. Gordon

01

WHY DO BAD THINGS HAPPEN TO GOOD PEOPLE?

The heaven, even the heavens, are the LORD'S: but
the earth hath he given to the children of men.

PSALMS 115:16

The concept that many people have that God is in control is one of the most damaging doctrines being promoted these days. If God is in control, why do innocent children get shot in school? Why do babies get aborted for convenience' sake? Why is the media allowed to disseminate endless lies and propaganda? Why do tornados and hurricanes kill people and destroy livelihoods? The list could go on and on. God is sovereign, but in His sovereignty He put man in charge of the earth (Psalms 115:16). Originally Adam was in charge of this world; God's plan was to have Adam and Eve rule the world in partnership with Him. Things were wonderful until Adam and Eve disobeyed God by being manipulated by Satan. That's when Satan became the god of this world.

In whom the god of this world hath blinded the minds of them which believe not, lest the light of the glorious gospel of Christ, who is the image of God, should shine unto them.

2 Corinthians 4:4

Satan has now become the god of this world. This is why bad things happen to good people and why we see so much evil in the world.

Often God gets blamed for all the things the devil does. This would make sense if God were in control. The truth of the matter is that usually God only gets involved when He's invited into the affairs of men. That's why our prayers are so important. Through prayer and living godly lives, we can limit Satan's ability to steal, kill, and destroy. We can bring God's will to pass which is the more abundant life.

The thief cometh not, but for to steal, and to kill, and to destroy: I am come that they might have life, and that they might have it more abundantly.

John 10:10

Also, bad things can be averted by acquiring a close relationship with God because He will lead you to avoid situations only He sees. Learning to hear His voice becomes vital.

If God got His way, everyone would be saved and come unto the knowledge of the truth (1 Timothy 2:4). Obviously, that's not happening. God does not micromanage the planet. We have to make Jesus Lord; it's not automatic. God can make huge inroads into society if even a small remnant stands for Him. God gave man free will, and He goes along with our decisions—good or bad.

Ultimately God will have the final say. Why? Because in the long run, the greater power will come out ahead. The war was won at the resurrection of Jesus Christ. There will be a new heaven and earth one day, and evil will be gone forever.

Many people have turned against God because of unfair circumstances in this life, thinking God was in control. But as we have seen, this idea is erroneous. The standard for God's love is not the circumstances in this life, but God sending Jesus to die for us.

> *But God commendeth his love toward us, in that,*
> *while we were yet sinners, Christ died for us.*
> Romans 5:8

> *Hereby perceive we the love of God, because he laid*
> *down his life for us: and we ought to lay down our*
> *lives for the brethren.*
> 1 John 3:16

> *In this was manifested the love of God toward us,*
> *because that God sent his only begotten Son into the*
> *world, that we might live through him.*
> 1 John 4:9

Don't spend your time trying to figure out why all the bad things happened in negative circumstances. You will just build unbelief and despair and become ineffective. We're in a war. Now we see through a glass darkly. When Christ comes back we'll understand all.

The most sensible thing we can do in this life is to stay put with God and continue with Him no matter what happens. If we quit on God, there's no hope; if we continue with God there's always hope.

God will have the final say. Justice will be meted out in the judgments of the future. In the meantime, stay in the fight with God. God bless you.

02

WHY LIVE ACCORDING TO GOD'S STANDARDS?

The fear of the LORD is clean, enduring forever: the judgments of the LORD are true and righteous altogether. Moreover by them is thy servant warned: and in keeping of them there is great reward.

PSALMS 19:9,11

When I was in my twenties, I was involved with a Christian ministry that started out really good. I believe it saved my life. Later on, however, like other ministres I've heard about, they began to compromise on God's standard of sexual purity.

I'm very thankful for the Bible knowledge I learned during those years including the operation of the Holy Spirit manifestations. However, the sexual sin led to the ministry's downfall. Many people were badly hurt, and some even gave up their commitment to Christ. Lives were ruined.

I thought if matters were brought into the open, the ministry could be restored. We confronted the leadership on this matter, and the result was that, along with many others, we were kicked out. Our intention was to help them repent and move on with the things of God. Fortunately for Mary and myself, our commitment to God was strong enough that we were able to pick up the pieces of our lives and move on with Him. We found that the people whose primary commitment was to the ministry went down with the ship. Those who were committed to God first were able to get back on their feet and grow with God.

Several years later, I was conversing with a pastor friend of mine from the same background. Apparently, I had been influenced by the compromised thinking because I suggested that fornication might actually be okay in some situations. I pointed out that in our day and time, people don't generally get married before their late teens or early twenties. In Bible times they got married in their early teens. He made a statement that hit me right between the eyes. God does not change His standards because of culture. He was absolutely right.

God sees things from a spiritual point of view. He knows that fornication and adultery are open doors for the devil to get in and destroy people's lives. If you give the devil an inch he'll take a mile.

God doesn't make rules to restrict our freedom. His precepts are there to keep us free and prosperous. If we break God's rules we open the door to the enemy to rack and ruin our lives. The destruction will then spread to others and become epidemic.

This applies to all of God's standards, not just sexual sin. America at one time was morally pure to a much greater extent. Look where we are today. Bribery, greed, lust for power, false accusations, among other ungodly activities are common and accepted.

God always offers mercy and restoration when there is repentance for our sins. Sometimes people need deliverance from demonic oppression before they are able to avoid sin. But if we continue in willful sin and purposely defy God and don't repent, there will be a great price to pay now and for eternity.

> For if we sin wilfully after that we have received the knowledge of the truth, there remaineth no more sacrifice for sins,
>
> But a certain fearful looking for of judgment and fiery indignation, which shall devour the adversaries.
>
> Hebrews 10:26, 27

2 Samuel 12 depicts when the prophet Nathan confronted David regarding his affair with Bathsheba as well as arranging for her husband to be killed. The consequences were strife and destruction in his personal family.

Although David repented and was forgiven, the consequences were set in motion and still occurred. One son, Amnon raped his half-sister Tamar, and Absolom her full brother killed Amnon. Absolom later tried to usurp the authority of the kingdom which forced his father David into exile. Joab killed Absolom, and David was restored to the throne.

Another son, Adonijah, later tried to take rulership as heir, but David had promised that to Solomon, a son by Bathsheba.

Some consequences still occur even after the sin is forgiven, but sometimes they can be averted.

Certain sins were punishable by death in the Old Testament, but they are not treated that way today. These sins include homosexuality, beastiality, and witchcraft to name a few. Why? Because they are demonically inspired. Before Jesus, casting out demons was almost unheard of. The only way to limit the power of those demons was to kill the person in whom they dwelt.

Today people can get delivered from these demons and live successful lives. I personally know of five incidents where homosexuals were delivered and able to have successful heterosexual marriages.

If we follow God's standards we will be protected and live a prosperous life. If we break His standards there are consequences. No one lived God's standards perfectly except our Lord Jesus Christ. But we can get closer and closer to living God's standards as we stay in the battle and try.

God has limitless love, forgiveness, and mercy for those who desire to please Him. All He asks of us is to do our best and we will live the best possible life here on earth. We will also get rewards in eternity.

03

WHY FORGIVE?

And his lord was wroth, and delivered him to the tormentors,
till he should pay all that was due unto him. So likewise
shall my heavenly Father do also unto you, if ye from your
hearts forgive not every one his brother their trespasses.

MATTHEW 18:34,35

Several years ago I heard a minister whom I knew fairly well share the following true story. A lady was losing her eyesight and continually getting worse. She had been in an abusive relationship with her former husband. Although she was safe from him now, she carried a lot of hatred, bitterness, and resentment towards him.

As the minister was praying, the Holy Spirit brought up the issue of unforgiveness. The minister asked her if she were willing to forgive her ex-husband. That set her off, and she exclaimed, "Absolutely not, after what he's done?" He then asked her if the man gave her $1 million would she forgive him. After a bit of thought, she replied, "Yes." Then he informed her that the guy certainly owed her at least that much, but she was holding on to the I.O.U. in her own hand.

She finally agreed to forgive him, and her eyesight started to improve immediately! I believe her vision was totally restored.

I've had a lot of training in a field called inner healing and deliverance. The most common thing blocking deliverance for people is unforgiveness. I believe that the tormentors of Matthew 18 are demons that afflict the mind and body. I can't guarantee that if you forgive you'll get the immediate results this lady got, but I can guarantee that if you hold on to unforgiveness, the door is open to Satan to attack your mind with bad thoughts. Many times these lingering thoughts will bring on physical sickness. I know this from personal experience.

> To whom ye forgive any thing, I forgive also: for if I forgave any thing, to whom I forgave it, for your sakes forgave I it in the person of Christ; Lest Satan should get an advantage of us: for we are not ignorant of his devices.
>
> 2 Corinthians 2:10, 11

Forgiveness is a decision that sets you free. It never was meant to be a form of excusing the offender. It's designed to bring freedom to your own heart. When you decide to forgive, you are giving God permission to get involved. It doesn't mean the emotional trauma will necessarily be fixed right away, but at least God can start the healing process.

Many times there's unforgiveness toward God as well as yourself. This also needs attention. Forgiveness gets easier the more you practice it.

When you choose to forgive, you're getting out of God's way so He can handle the situation.

> ... *Vengeance is mine; I will repay, saith the Lord.*
> Romans 12:19b

God sees the motives of the heart; He's the only one that can judge righteously. In certain situations, you may still need to take the offender to court to get restitution, but in addition, you must make the decision to forgive. Often your forgiveness helps clear the air for the offender as well, but for certain, it will help you. How peaceful are you when you dwell on bitterness or resentment? Holding on to unforgiveness is like swallowing poison and hoping the other person gets sick or dies. Most of the time, the other person is unaffected while you're back home suffering. In some cases, the offender may scorn you, not caring in the least whether you forgive him or not.

Let's practice forgiveness and be happier and healthier people.

04

IT'S NOT HOPELESS; THINGS CAN CHANGE

Now the God of hope fill you with all joy and peace in believing, that ye may abound in hope, through the power of the Holy Ghost.

ROMANS 15:13

've heard of people asking about the horrific events that have bombarded them from the news. "How could God allow that to happen?" In the times we live, God put man in charge.

> *The heaven, even the heavens, are the LORD'S: but the earth hath he given to the children of men.*
>
> Psalms 115:16

If we kick God out, we are left to our own devices which will lead to destruction and chaos. We have taken God out of schools, government, etc., so we are reaping a bad harvest.

I have studied the whole Bible for decades. When Israel turned away from God, things would get worse and worse. When they would cry out to God for help, repent, and get Him involved, He always did. Many times things changed quickly when enough people sought His help. It's the same here in America. If we keep turning away from God, things will get worse and worse. If we turn back to Him, things will get better.

You can't legislate goodness into peoples' hearts; it can't be legislated. If we turn back to Him, He can change hearts and circumstances. As bad as things look, it's not hopeless. Let's turn back to God and watch things change for the better.

05

FROM DEPRESSION TO PURPOSE

Where there is no vision, the people perish.

PROVERBS 29:18A

I came from a broken home. Although I was never abused, my parents were always arguing when they were together. My mother was in and out of the hospital with depression her entire life. I grew up with very similar problems.

From age five until I became an avid Christian at twenty-one, I can't remember one day when I wasn't depressed. Some days were worse than others.

My father never realized I had a problem with depression until I had a discussion with him when I was in my thirties. He thought I was just like him, very strong emotionally.

When I was in high school, I started writing letters to God saying, "If You exist, You will have to get me out of this state of mind." I didn't know how much longer I could take it. Even though I got good grades, was good in sports, was good-looking, and had a steady girlfriend, I was sinking more and more into despair.

When I was in college I got involved with a non-denominational, charismatic Christian ministry which I thought would help. I accepted Christ, and three days later I received what people call the baptism of the Holy Spirit. I spoke in tongues. I knew something supernatural had taken place; I couldn't deny it.

For a year after that, I claimed to be a Christian, but I didn't want to give up fornication. I reached a point of desperation and decided to give up willful sin and wholeheartedly follow Jesus. That's when things started to change—slowly.

I realized the main reason for my depression was that I believed life was futile. Why strive to succeed if all we do is live and die? I didn't think the effort was worth it. When I fully submitted to living for Christ, things changed. I now had purpose!

Not only was I promised eternal life, but I would be rewarded eternally on top of that for living for Christ now.

> *For God is not unrighteous to forget your work and labour of love, which ye have shewed toward his name.*
> Hebrews 6:10a

There are rewards, crowns, and prizes available in the future for our stand for God right now. Also, we have God to help us navigate and be successful here in this life. Such a deal!

My life had been in a hole of depression for so long that I had a lot of baggage. I didn't change overnight, but instead of things quickly getting worse, things slowly got better.

I did student teaching in my last year of college. I don't believe I would have had the confidence to do it if I hadn't become a determined, committed Christian. However, I actually did rather well as a student teacher.

After committing my life to Christ almost fifty years ago, I've had many ups and downs. I was raised a nominal Jew, but I've been an avid Christian since 1974. I've had very trying circumstances along the way, but I've never quit on God, and He has always brought me through.

I also had supernatural proof that what I believed, was true. Accepting Christ was only the beginning. Since then I've seen hundreds of miraculous healings. Personally, I've had visions and supernatural dreams; I prophesy frequently; and I've witnessed other types of miracles.

Every time the enemy tries to break you, he's taking a risk that he will make you stronger. Whenever you face a crisis and allow God to bring you through to the other side, you get added strength to walk for Him.

Without Christ and in my depression, I doubt I would have lived beyond thirty. But I am now seventy-two with a successful business, a good marriage, and health. I still play tennis a couple of times a week in nice weather. Also, my wife and I have been able through ministry to help thousands of people over the years.

Let me digress. I have often heard Christians try to motivate people by declaring that without Christ they would end up in hell. This would never have worked for me. As far as I was concerned, I was already in my own hell. Why would I want to know about a God so cruel that He would allow people to go through hell in this life and then send them to hell for eternity? Not me! It only drove me farther away. I wasn't interested.

Romans 2:4 says it's the goodness of God that leads a man to repentance. If the reason you are serving God is to avoid hell, you don't understand salvation by grace. Don't read what I'm not saying, but that's not the motivation God wants for you. He wants to prove Himself to you NOW in this life. If you are open to the supernatural you will give God the opportunity He desires, to show you His power. This builds confidence and boldness.

There does come a point for those who continually defy God to realize that severe consequences await them if they don't repent. Fortunately, God is extremely patient and extends extravagant mercy to people. Generally speaking, people in today's culture need to know God's love for them. Let that be their starting point, not the fear of going to hell.

Regardless of your motivation, let's continue serving God in this life. It's the best thing going now and also for eternity. You can't lose.

> *Wherefore seeing we also are compassed about with so great a cloud of witnesses, let us lay aside every weight, and the sin which doth so easily beset us, and let us run with patience the race that is set before us.*
> Hebrews 12:1

06

WHAT DID I GET MYSELF INTO WHEN I BECAME A CHRISTIAN?

*For our light affliction, which is but for a moment, worketh
for us a far more exceeding and eternal weight of glory.*

2 CORINTHIANS 4:17

When I first became a Christian, I was attracted by the promise that I would find the power to overcome my emotional and physical problems. I had a bad case of depression and some painful digestive problems due to anxiety. My mother had been in and out of the hospital with depression her entire life. She had a lot of medical treatment and psychotherapy to help her.

I had very similar problems to her, although I never did any of the medical stuff. I realized as I got older, my negative attitude was rooted in hopelessness.

> *That at that time ye were without Christ, being aliens from the commonwealth of Israel, and*

strangers from the covenants of promise, having no hope, and without God in the world:

Ephesians 2:12

The message of hope I got from Christianity was true. However, some churches entice people to become Christians by teaching that Christianity is a life of ease with all desires being met. That's a false message. The Bible says that all who desire to lead godly lives will suffer persecution.

Yea, and all that will live godly in Christ Jesus shall suffer persecution.

2 Timothy 3:12

We are told by Jesus Himself that we will be hated by the world. Also, Paul says in Romans 7:24: "O wretched man that I am! Who shall deliver me from the body of this death?" The internal struggle he had was grueling.

When we become Christians and really attempt to live for God, hell takes note. Many times our personal problems and other issues will increase for a time while we are learning to fight God's way with His power. But God stays with us even then. He promises that we are "more than conquerors" (Romans 8:37). We won't be tempted more than we can handle at any time (1 Corinthians 10:13). Our weapons are "mighty through God to the pulling down of strongholds" (2 Corinthians 10:4).

When you become a Christian, you make Jesus Lord. You are no longer allowed to have your own opinions about topics covered in scripture. You must align your thinking with the standards presented in the Bible. This includes things like sexuality, finances, conversations, etc. God's Word now becomes your standard for truth. Don't get into fruitless arguments with unbelievers about topics addressed in scripture. If they want to know what you believe, simply direct them to the Bible.

After I got saved, it took me a year of being miserable before I really made the decision to adopt God's standards regarding premarital sex. Once I did, I started overcoming years of depression, confusion, selfishness, and sickness. The decision was instant, but the victory took time.

When you really decide to make Jesus Lord, in some ways, the fight has just begun. But if you remain unsaved, you are destined for eternal death. If you get saved and go your own way, you will not have any victories in this life, and won't have any rewards in the future. But if you really make Jesus Lord, you can have righteousness, peace, and joy now. See Romans 14:17.

In my case, coming from depression, one of my biggest struggles has been to stay positive. Since world news tends to be negative, I have literally divorced myself from listening most of the time.

Others I know who had a positive outlook on life have struggled in other areas. I know one person who dramatically had to work on feeling loved.

If I didn't have God in my life, I believe I would have left the planet by the age of thirty. But now I'm seventy-two, and I've had a fruitful life to this day.

Being a Christian and making Jesus Lord is not easy, but the alternative is devastating. We were born into a war between good and evil. Nobody escapes.

Let's continue to grow in our relationship with the Lord. The rewards now and in the future are well worth it.

07

OCCUPY TILL I COME

*And he called his ten servants, and delivered them ten
pounds, and said unto them, Occupy till I come.*

LUKE 19:13

Several times in recent years I've come across Christians who have given up on America, even among church leadership. I've met some who don't vote anymore, thinking it's useless since America is doomed anyway. Is this the proper response to the crisis we're experiencing in the world today?

What did Jesus mean in Luke where he said, "Occupy till I come"? I believe He meant we are to use the gifts and talents He's given us to influence the world as much and as long as we can for the kingdom of God. We're supposed to continue and possibly increase our influence on society in light of the turmoil today.

No one knows when Christ is coming back. From my extensive studies, I can see that the technology is in place for all the events described in the Book of Revelation to take place. However, no one knows exactly when Christ will come back. Some say things are continually going to get worse. Some very prominent ministers say we're on the verge of a great awakening. I choose to believe things can at least temporarily get better.

One thing is for sure. If the body of Christ stops fighting for God's values, the quality of life will get more and more degraded. If we continue in the fight with God, our personal lives will improve and position us to change society for the better. A small remnant standing for God can make a huge difference. Leviticus 26:8 says, "And five of you shall chase an hundred, and an hundred of you shall put ten thousand to flight: and your enemies shall fall before you by the sword."

One of the devil's tactics is to wear down God's people.

> *And he shall speak great words against the most High, and shall wear out the saints of the most High, and think to change times and laws ….*
>
> Daniel 7:25

The wearing down of God's people is not necessarily by physical abuse, but rather by mental abuse, using the words sent to our ears. That's a primary reason for the corrupt news media. Be careful what you listen to.

I believe if we live in this country, it's our responsibility to vote whether there's fraud or not. As Christians, our responsibility is to influence culture for God as much as we can. We all have a sphere of influence. Don't underestimate what you can do.

Let's stay in the fight and occupy till He comes. We'll have rewards now and in the future, and we may pull some people out of the fire.

> *And of some have compassion, making a difference:*
> *And others save with fear, pulling them out of the*
> *fire ....*
>
> Jude 22, 23

08

CAN I OPERATE IN THE SUPERNATURAL?

*Verily, verily, I say unto you, He that believeth on me,
the works that I do shall he do also; and greater works
than these shall he do; because I go unto my Father.*

JOHN 14:12

Why is Harry Potter so popular? Why do people enjoy movies about witches and warlocks? Why do people get into the occult? I believe it's because there's an innate hunger in human beings to operate in the supernatural. We want to control our destiny rather than be controlled by the world.

God originally put Adam and Eve in charge of this earth. They operated supernaturally as long as they stayed under God's authority. At that time Adam was in charge of this world.

When Adam and Eve sinned, they lost their authority with God, and the devil became the god of this world, that is the god of this age. This is why the world is so evil today.

In the Old Testament God put Holy Spirit on certain individuals at times to bless His people and show His power. These people did operate in the supernatural, and they did perform great things for God. Note Sampson, Moses, Elijah, Elisha, and others. The spirit that God put on them, however, was conditional to being obedient to Himself. King Saul had the spirit and lost it because of his disobedience. After David sinned, he prayed to God not to take his Holy Spirit away.

Today, however, when we accept Christ, we are born again of incorruptible seed (1 Peter 1:21). God's spirit is sealed in us (Ephesians 1:13). We can't lose it. We can ignore the spirit, but it's still there.

How do you know a car has a battery without looking under the hood? If the car starts, if the horn honks, if the electric windows work, you know the battery is there even if you don't see it.

How do you know you have the Holy Spirit? 1 Corinthians 12:7-10 lists nine supernatural manifestations or evidences of the spirit. Most people call them gifts, but they are not. If you read 1 Corinthians 12:4-7 in the old King James Version, you will see that the manifestation of the spirit is contrasted with gifts, administrations, and operations. Every person has the potential to utilize these manifestations if he's born again.

Upon a casual reading of the verses, it may appear that one person has one manifestation, and another person has another. The Greek text as well as my personal experience indicates every believer has the potential to operate in all of them. I have operated repeatedly in all nine over the years.

Think of the manifestations like a clump of grapes where the gift, Holy Spirit, is the clump, and each manifestation is one of the grapes. You don't get one grape; you get the whole clump.

I am not saying that if you don't operate in the supernatural, you are not saved. You are saved when you accept Christ (Romans 10:9&10). God can still give you assurance of your salvation, but generally, you can't operate with God's supernatural power without the gift of the Holy Spirit. The Book of Acts illustrates that people believed the apostles because of the supernatural things they did.

The devil can counterfeit much of what God does. Simon the sorcerer operated in demonic power and deceived the people for many years. When people function in demonic power, the man gets glorified, rather than God. People said of Simon, "This man is the great power of God." Also, God does not possess and control one's free will. The devil always does. Simon believed because he could not reproduce the magnitude of what Philip was doing.

There's a doctrine called cessationism which has permeated much of the church. It says the supernatural power of God ended when we got the Scriptures we have today. I believe this is a deception promulgated by Satan to rob the church of power.

God can and does at times sovereignly lead people into the manifestation of the spirit. I had a customer once who wanted to speak in tongues. She had a dream that she was actually doing it, and woke up finding herself speaking in tongues for the first time. In my experience, most people operate in the supernatural power of God after being instructed by somebody who already did. That's how I learned.

The more I practice, the better I get. Even in the Old Testament, there were schools of the prophets to teach how the prophetic worked. I personally would never have stayed put as a Christian if I hadn't operated supernaturally. Once I did, I could never deny the reality of God and be honest with myself.

For many, if they don't operate in God's power, they will migrate to the power of Satan. This will cause destruction in their own lives as well as others. The devil's whole ministry is to steal, to kill, and to destroy (John 10:10b).

I realize this article may be stretching some of you a bit. I love and accept fellow Christians even if they don't agree with me. However, I would like to challenge you to seek God's supernatural power. It will increase your faith, and your walk, and enable you to be a more effective witness. It will also make your walk with God more exciting.

09

EVANGELIZING THE WORLD SUPERNATURALLY

*And the people with one accord gave heed
unto those things which Philip spake, hearing
and seeing the miracles which he did.*

ACTS 8:6

My wife, Mary, and I went into a Middle Eastern deli several years ago in Harrisburg PA. Mary had an impression that the man preparing our food had sore feet and asked him, "Do your feet hurt?" He shockingly answered, "Yes." Then she asked if she could pray for him, and he agreed. She prayed and commanded the pain to leave from his feet, and to his amazement, the pain left immediately. "How did you do that? How did you do that?" the man excitedly asked. At that point, I got involved in the conversation, and as we spoke, I began *prophesying* to him some very specific things going on in his family, and how God wanted to help him. He was flabbergasted to say the least. He wondered how I could "know" all these things about him. The reality was that I did not know anything about him, but as I spoke, God downloaded to me what to say. Then I asked him if he were Christian, and he replied, "No, I am Muslim." That was Mary's cue to give him a large dose of Jesus.

Meanwhile, another man preparing food behind the same counter got to see and hear the whole thing. Assuming he was also Muslim, I can now claim that two Muslims experienced the power of our God firsthand!

I was born and raised a Jew. In 1973 I got involved with a ministry that believed in what people call the gifts of the spirit found in 1 Corinthians 12:8-10. I had seen people speak in tongues, interpret, and prophesy in their meetings. That intrigued me. But when I spoke in tongues three days after I accepted Christ, that sealed it for me. This thing is real!

I don't believe the deli worker in Harrisburg would have paid too much attention to us if we had walked in there handing out tracts and telling him how much God loved him. But when his feet got healed, and I read his mail, that got his attention.

I, being a Jew never would have become a Christian if I had never seen anything supernatural. But when I myself experienced it, that convinced me. And now I've been an avid Christian for fifty years.

There's nothing wrong with handing out tracts, offering free hot dogs and drinks, and telling people God loves them, but there needs to be more if we're going to impact this hardened world.

And these signs shall follow them that believe; In my name shall they cast out devils; they shall speak with new tongues; They shall take up serpents; and if they drink any deadly thing, it shall not hurt them; they shall lay hands on the sick, and they shall recover.

Mark 16:17, 18

For the most part, if we're going to reach communists, Muslims, Jews, etc., we need to have the supernatural along with love and preaching. There are even Christian groups that deny the supernatural power of God still operates today. That's a lie! Supernatural healings and other manifestations of God's power happen regularly. I personally have witnessed hundreds of such incidents, especially over the last eight or nine years.

Jesus either preached and then demonstrated the power of God, or He demonstrated the power of God followed by preaching. We're supposed to follow Him.

… many believed in his name, when they saw the miracles which he did.

John 2:23b

And they went forth, and preached every where, the Lord working with them, and confirming the word with signs following. Amen.

Mark 16:20

Note also I Corinthians 2:4 which reads, "And my speech and my preaching was not with enticing words of man's wisdom, but in demonstration of the Spirit and of power"! The supernatural is supposed to be present to confirm the Word of God.

We need the supernatural power of God more than ever in this day and time. Every Christian has the potential to operate in the nine supernatural manifestations of God's power. Sometimes God will sovereignly teach people how, but in my own experience as well as others, we were trained by other experienced Christians how to <u>activate</u> God's power. You also can do this.

Let's step up to the plate. and be the bold witnesses we can be. God and the world need us. We desperately must display God's supernatural power to evangelize the world.

10

DEFINITIONS OF THE MANIFESTATIONS OF THE SPIRIT

For to one is given by the Spirit the word of wisdom; to another the word of knowledge by the same Spirit; To another faith by the same Spirit; to another the gifts of healing by the same Spirit; To another the working of miracles; to another prophecy; to another discerning of spirits; to another divers kinds of tongues; to another the interpretation of tongues.

1 CORINTHIANS 12:8-10

Let's take a deeper look at each of these spiritual manifestations we spoke about in the last chapter. In my studies, I came across detailed definitions for each one. I will present them here. Please note, they did not originate with me; however, I have altered them slightly based on my own use of them.

Speaking in tongues is speaking a language unknown to the speaker through the power of the Holy Spirit. The person speaks, but Holy Spirit gives the words. It's either a language of men or of angels. When it's a language of men, it's possible that someone else present understands.

Interpretation of tongues is speaking the gist of what that person just spoke in tongues. It is not a word-for-word translation, nor does it imply the person was given a translation, because the interpretation is spoken by inspiration as he speaks. It can either be in the first or third person. Interpretation of tongues serves the same function as prophecy except that the tongues is a sign to the unbeliever. Generally, the inspired interpretation is spoken by the one who just spoke in tongues.

Prophecy is speaking inspired words from the Holy Spirit for the purpose of one or more of the following: edification, exhortation, and comfort. It can't be outside of these categories. It can either be to a group or to an individual. It can also be in the first or third person. Note: this is not to be confused with the ministry of a prophet. Foretelling is generally limited to the five-fold gift ministry of a prophet. Also, any foretelling of negative events must have redeeming value: i.e., to get prepared or to avoid the situation.

Word of knowledge is information revealed by the Holy Spirit that could not be known naturally.

Word of wisdom is the knowledge of what to do about a situation as revealed by the Holy Spirit. It often accompanies word of knowledge.

Discerning of spirits is receiving knowledge via the Holy Spirit determining whether demons, angels, or Holy Spirit are present. If demons are present, Holy Spirit may reveal what kind they are and whether or not you may cast them out. *Discerning of spirits* is not the gift of discernment which means acuteness of judgment. This in itself is not a manifestation of the spirit.

The manifestation of faith is the supernatural ability through Holy Spirit to believe to have something to come to pass. If you are operating in this manifestation, it absolutely will take place.

Gifts of healing is bringing healing to pass supernaturally. If it's instantaneous it's a miracle. Not all healing is instantaneous; sometimes a period of time is involved.

Working of miracles is bringing things to pass supernaturally.

11

MIRACLES I'VE SEEN

And they went forth, and preached every where,
the Lord working with them, and confirming
the word with signs following. Amen.

MARK 16:20

I walked into a church to tune their big grand piano. I noticed the praise dance team was practicing, and there was a somewhat sad-looking girl sitting in a pew. I got into a conversation with her, and she told me she used to be on the praise dance team, but she had extreme pain in her leg and couldn't dance anymore. I asked if I could pray for her. She agreed, so I prayed a few short prayers for her leg, but nothing seemed to happen. I told her, "I release you in faith," and went about tuning the piano.

The next year when I returned to take care of their annual tuning, she happened to see me. She ran up to me and excitedly exclaimed, "You're the one that prayed for my leg, and it got healed. I'm now dancing again with the praise team." Then I was as excited as she and thanked the Lord.

Several years ago I was in West Virginia tuning pianos for some long-term clients. One lady informed me she couldn't hear a thing out of one ear because of an ear infection. At that time I was personally suffering from mild depression and feeling a bit down. I had learned, however, that even if I wasn't doing well myself, I could still pray for others, and they could get healed.

I asked her if I could pray for her, and she agreed. Then I asked if I could put my hand on her ear, and she agreed to that too. I then commanded her hearing to come back in the name of Jesus Christ, and her hearing was totally restored. I ran into her several days later, and she said her hearing had been fine ever since I prayed for her.

Another time, I was on a job at a Salvation Army post. The captain had been in a motorcycle wreck several years previous and still had back pain. I prayed for his back and then had him test it. He said the pain was gone.

Then I sat him down in a pew and put his back straight against the back of the pew. I lifted his legs so they stuck straight out in front of him. One leg was visibly shorter than the other. When I prayed I watched it grow out until the legs were even. We both were very grateful for what God had done.

Recently, I was at my doctor's office waiting to get blood drawn. I heard another patient in the waiting room talk about having neuropathy (no feeling) in her feet. I recounted to her another incident where I had prayed over the phone for a friend who also had neuropathy in both her legs and feet. As I prayed, she felt heat start in her legs, and it slowly moved down all the way through her feet, and all the feeling came back.

I then asked if I could pray for her, and she said, "Yes." Guess what happened when I prayed. A heat started in her legs also and moved through her feet exactly how I had described my previous experience. All her feeling was restored as well. She was shocked. Yay, God.

Five years ago, my printer/copier quit working. I was on the phone with the company as one of their technicians walked me through several steps before determining it would cost more to fix than to buy another one. The problem with that was I'd just stocked up on several of those very expensive ink cartridges. I called my wife to the room; we laid hands on the printer and commanded it to work. It still works to this day.

Two years ago, I had to give up trying to fix my old lawn mower, and I opened a new cheap one in the box. I put it together, gassed it up, checked the oil, primed it, and pulled the cord. Nothing. I pulled it about 20 times without success. So I called my wife on the phone and told her we needed to pray for the new lawn mower. It didn't start when I pulled the cord the first time, but on the second pull it fired right up, and I mowed the lawn.

The next time I needed to mow, again, it wouldn't start. So I called Mary from my phone to pray. and then it started, but not until the second pull. Throughout the entire season, this happened about five times. After prayer, it wouldn't start on the first pull, but it always started on the second.

Don't ask me why that is; I have no idea.

One time I was tuning a piano where the lady was in the process of restoring her home after a house fire. Her beautiful white carpet had just been cleaned and was still covered with plastic.

I needed to replace six chipped ivory keytops. To loosen the old glue, I had to heat the keytop until it was very hot. When I pried one particular ivory to remove it, it flipped up into the air and landed somewhere. I frantically searched for it knowing it would melt the plastic covering and also put a burn hole in her lovely carpet. It should have landed at my feet, but it seemed to have disappeared.

Then I glanced into my tool case, and there it was. I sure was relieved that it had done no damage, but how could it have gotten there? I was dumbfounded; that case was six feet away. I'm convinced an angel protected me from an expensive, embarrassing situation. It was still warm when I picked it up.

Last year I was teaching a group of twenty people at a church how to minister healing and get results. I always find a volunteer to demonstrate God's power. A lady came to the front of the class who had pain throughout her body. I began to pray and laid my hand on her shoulder. A picture came to my mind of a serpent whose tail was in her belly and whose head was in her head. God was showing me that her problem was demonic. I started calling out the demon, and after a little while, it left and so did her pain.

On another occasion, my wife couldn't find her hearing aids. We had been on a trip and thought we had put them in a small case she carried. We both searched the whole house including that case many times and hadn't found them. They cost over $4000, so I certainly didn't want to lose them.

Furthermore, we were going to a Bible teaching that evening, and I really wanted Mary to be able to hear the minister. We had prayed for the hearing aids to show up. It was time to leave, and I said to Mary, "I'm going to check that case one more time before leaving." I went up to the third floor, put my hand in that case, and felt the hearing aids. I believe God put them there supernaturally.

In someone's home where I was tuning a piano, I carried on a conversation with a contractor doing some work there. He had been an avid believer at one time, but had turned his back on God. He actually had been a student at a well-known Christian university.

He was trying to talk me out of my faith, but I countered by telling him some of the healing miracles I've seen. He tried to tell me it was the power of positive thinking. I suggested he tell that to the lady who got healed of neuropathy, or the one who got her hearing restored, and so forth. He soon quit talking, realizing he wasn't going to get anywhere with me.

These are a few of the miraculous experiences I've had. In the last ten years, I've seen hundreds of healings and other manifestations of God's power.

A good friend of mine who was also a minister once said, "You can argue with my doctrine, but you can't argue with my testimony." How true that is.

I don't have a big ministry by the world's standards. I'm a normal human who believes God. Many people say I have a special anointing. I believe the reason I see a lot of miracles is that I pray for a lot of people expecting God to move. If you never pray for any sick people, don't expect to see miraculous healings.

If you try it and pray consistently, I believe the results will mushroom. That's the way it was for me as well as others who have experienced what I have.

Some people have told me they don't need to see miraculous things in order to believe. To me that's a religious mindset used as an excuse not to step out of their comfort zone. God would love to confirm His Word for you with signs following. Having concrete examples builds confidence rather than having to take everything "on faith."

Give God a chance to prove Himself to you.

12

HOW POWERFUL IS THE DEVIL?

But if our gospel be hid, it is hid to them that are lost:
In whom the god of this world hath blinded the minds of
them which believe not, lest the light of the glorious gospel
of Christ, who is the image of God, should shine unto them.

1 CORINTHIANS 4:3,4

If you listen to the news or even listen to the conversations of most Christians, you would think the devil is extremely powerful, and God is puny. I guarantee you that the news media is bent on magnifying the evil things Satan does and minimizing the goodness of God. Satan is called the god of this world, or more accurately, this age.

He is also called the prince of the power of the air in Ephesians 2:2. God owns the world, not the devil (Psalms 24:1). However, the devil runs the systems of this world by corruption and lies.

The devil is a created being. He is not all-powerful. God is. Elisha had a proper perspective of things in 2 Kings 6:17. In that record they were surrounded by the enemy and it looked as if they were doomed. Gehazi was petrified. Then Elisha prayed for his eyes to be enlightened as he declared there were more with them than with the enemy.

Then Gehazi looked and saw chariots of fire surrounding the enemy. What he actually saw was angels. We have two-thirds of the angels on our side in addition to the Godhead. We outnumber the enemy by more than two to one. We definitely have the advantage.

The devil and his angels are spirit beings and are far greater than unsaved men according to 2 Peter 2:11. You're not going to beat them with assault weapons or nukes.

> *Whereas angels, which are greater in power and might, bring not railing accusation against them before the Lord.*
>
> 2 Peter 2:11

However, man with God on his side is infinitely bigger than the devil, who knows he lost the war at the resurrection of Jesus Christ. He just doesn't want you to know.

We give power to the spirit realm by agreement. Agreeing with negative declarations will empower Satan. On the other hand, agreeing with God empowers angels.

God can defeat Satan with a very small remnant. Look at Gideon, David and Goliath, Samson, or many of Israel's battles in the Old Testament. Nothing is too hard for God.

But we must do things His way and agree with Him. Let's agree with God and win some battles.

13

THE POWER OF WORDS

Death and life are in the power of the tongue: and they that love it shall eat the fruit thereof.

PROVERBS 18:21

This theme Scripture in The Message reads, "Words kill, words give life; they're either poison or fruit—you choose." Whether you realize it or not, you are giving direction to your life by the words you speak, by the conversations you entertain.

When I was a kid I was very insecure. I used to cover up my insecurity by telling dirty jokes and making crude comments when I was with my friends. I remember in ninth grade I was with several friends having a normal conversation when I made a crude, off-the-wall comment, and immediately the conversation went down the drain. Everyone joined in. We thought it was funny, but even then I noticed how quickly the conversation turned sour. I had initiated it; This was seven years before I met the Lord.

Numbers 13 and 14 record the incident when the twelve spies went in to check out the promised land. Ten spies came back with an "evil report," magnifying the strength of the enemy. Only two, Joshua and Caleb, came back with a "good report," magnifying the power of God. The report of the ten quickly caused a mutiny against God. God jumped in and stopped it, but that entire generation had to forfeit the enjoyment of the promised land. They wandered in the desert for 40 years, and the next generation went in under the leadership of Joshua.

Suppose all twelve had come back with a good report. Israel would have immediately gone into the promised land, but the discouraging words of the ten spies opened the door for spirits of discouragement, anger, and unbelief to infiltrate the camp. Their words quickly changed God's original plan of blessing. You can find more insight regarding this in chapter 32 of the Book of Numbers.

We live in a spiritual world. Spirits gain authority in our lives by words. If we speak words that line up with God's promises, we give God and His angels authority to carry out good things for us. If we speak the opposite, we empower Satan and his demons to wreak havoc.

In 1 Samuel 17, when David encountered Goliath, he refuted Goliath's threats with his own words of deliverance for Israel.

> *And the Philistine said unto David, Am I a dog, that thou comest to me with staves? And the Philistine cursed David by his gods.*

And the Philistine said to David, Come to me, and I will give thy flesh unto the fowls of the air, and to the beasts of the field.

Then said David to the Philistine, Thou comest to me with a sword, and with a spear, and with a shield: but I come to thee in the name of the LORD of hosts, the God of the armies of Israel, whom thou hast defied.

This day will the LORD deliver thee into mine hand; and I will smite thee, and take thine head from thee; and I will give the carcases of the host of the Philistines this day unto the fowls of the air, and to the wild beasts of the earth; that all the earth may know that there is a God in Israel.

And all this assembly shall know that the LORD saveth not with sword and spear: for the battle is the LORD'S, and he will give you into our hands.

1 Samuel 17:43-47

David's reliance was on God, and his words expressed that confidence. He slew Goliath which started the rout and defeat of the Philistines, thus securing freedom and victory for Israel.

We can see from this chapter's theme Scripture (Proverbs 18:21 above) that David's words gave God's invisible realm the authority to get involved. Many an argument can be started or avoided by words. Proverbs 25:11 says, "A word fitly spoken is like apples of gold in pictures of silver." From this, we see that godly words can heal and bring restoration.

Let's watch what we say. If we try to speak what God would have us say, we can make a great impact for the kingdom of God and improve life for both us and those we encounter.

Let's speak life over ourselves, our friends, and our nation.

14

CAN A CHRISTIAN BE POSSESSED?

And when he had called unto him his twelve disciples, he gave them power against unclean spirits, to cast them out, and to heal all manner of sickness and all manner of disease.

MATTHEW 10:1

About twenty years ago, Mary and I were trying to help a girl get off crack addiction. We had been ministering in a halfway house and had some experience with people who had substance abuse problems.

This girl was sitting in our living room in my white chair. We were good friends with her. She was a committed Christian who spoke in tongues and had been through a Bible school program.

I started praying for her. All of a sudden, she said, "Something inside me hates you." She then started calling me a bunch of horrible four-letter words. I recognized that those were demons in her. The words were coming from the demons, not her.

I was getting words in my mind like fear, hate, insecurity, murder, etc. God was showing me what demons were in her. I started calling the demons out by the names I was hearing in my mind.

I said, "Fear, I command you to come out in the name of Jesus Christ." The demons said, "We've been here a long time, and we're not coming out." I said, "Yes, you are."

I told the devils to shut up in the name of Jesus Christ and continued to call fear out. She felt pressure in her stomach. As I continued to call it out, the pressure moved up from her stomach to her throat, and finally came out her mouth. At one point she stood up and took a swing at me. I avoided the punch and commanded her to sit down in the name of Jesus Christ. She did. You see, it was the demons in her that caused her to rise in such an attack.

Once fear was gone, I called insecurity out. We went through the same scenario again. After one demon would leave through her mouth I'd call out another one. I ended up casting about eight demons out of her, and she felt much lighter and relieved once they were gone.

Recall that this girl was a good friend of ours. In her normal state, she was a fine believer. But these devils influenced her in her weak areas. Just because a person has demons, it does not make the person evil. Only the demons themselves are evil. Most of the time people are victims. This girl was a committed Christian who still had demonic problems. How can this happen?

The term *possessed* is a bad translation of a Greek word used to indicate *influenced by demons.* The field of inner healing and deliverance in which we were trained used the word *demonized* instead. Possession implies ownership.

When one is saved, he is owned by God, not the devil. There are three parts to a Christian: spirit, soul, and body. I don't believe a demon can mess with your spirit when a person is saved, but your soul and body are still vulnerable.

Your soul which is your mind, will, and emotions needs to be changed through your own efforts with God's help. Your body can be healed also as you renew your mind. The total salvation of the body will be evidenced when Christ returns. We are promised a new (spiritual) body at that time.

Ephesians 2:8 says, "For by grace are ye saved through faith; and that not of yourselves: it is the gift of God." However Philippians 2:12 says, "… work out your own salvation with fear and trembling." Is this a contradiction? I believe not!

In a class entitled, *The Salvations of Man,* I realized that spiritual salvation is different from the salvation of our souls. When one confesses Jesus as Lord and believes in his heart that God raised Him from the dead, that man is saved. That is spiritual salvation, and he has Holy Spirit living within. This is strictly by grace; it's a done deal. This is not the salvation of the soul. Soul salvation is what we must work out as stated in Philippians 2:12.

Demons can very well influence the soul and also the body. We know one lady who had a demon cast from her, and her MS was healed completely and immediately. In the example above, you saw how demons were cast out of an otherwise wonderful Christian girl.

After I got saved, I had to progressively get free from a spirit of depression that I grew up with. It was a lengthy fight and involved more than one demon. Demons have varying degrees of influence on people. Some may leave at the point of salvation; others may take considerable time and effort to overcome.

Demons prey on any kind of weakness. Any physical or mental weakness can open the door for a demon to enter. If demons are involved, psychiatry will only be able to treat the symptoms but not the cause. In such cases, people learn to cope rather than get delivered.

If a demon operates through a dysfunctional part of the brain, medication may numb that part of the brain so the demon can't operate. As soon as the medication wears off, the demon is back in business. I learned from Derek Prince Ministries that most long-standing emotional and mental problems people have are demonically based.

On the other hand, it is possible to have two cases with identical symptoms, but one is caused by a demon and the other has a physical cause. It will take the manifestations of discerning of spirits and word of knowledge to know the difference.

So, can a Christian be possessed? Not in the sense of ownership. A Christian's owner is God Himself. But demons certainly can and do afflict the minds and bodies of Christians.

Wherever you have weak areas in your life, don't resign yourself to the idea, "That's just me." You can become more and more free in Jesus Christ as you remain faithful to His Word, stay coachable, and stay in the fight.

15

THE DAY TWO WOMEN FOUGHT OVER ME
AND OTHER HUMOROUS EPISODES FROM A PIANO TUNER'S LIFE

A merry heart doeth good like a medicine ....
PROVERBS 17:22A

About ten years ago I went into the Alzheimer's unit of a local nursing home facility where there was a baby grand piano in the dining room for me to tune. I thought this would be a routine tuning. Little did I know!

I stripped the piano down (inserted the red felt-strip mutes) as usual and started tuning. While I was listening to the beats with the ding, ding, dings, an elderly lady approached me and said, in a rather irritated voice, "Can't you play anything better than that?" I attempted to explain that I was tuning the piano and that I would play her some songs when I was done.

This was to no avail whatsoever. She continued to heckle me. Finally, out of exasperation, I said, "Why don't you complain to the management; they hired me." She got up and walked into the middle of that dining room and yelled in a loud voice, "Help! Help!" One of the workers came and got her, and I assume, took her back to her room. About five minutes later she returned and actually sat down on the bench next to me. She bothered me to the extent that I could not work at all.

Another elderly lady who saw what was going on came to my rescue. These two women started yelling four-letter words back and forth at each other, and it appeared to me they might get into a fistfight. A couple of workers saw what was going on, broke up the argument, and took the two ladies away. I tell people, "That's the only time I can think of where two women were fighting over me."

Unfortunately, I never got to play any songs for that poor lady who didn't like my tuning. Now, whenever I tune at that facility, I go in late at night after everyone is asleep.

Here's another quick incident in a similar setting at another nursing home. I was tuning a piano in a large fellowship room. One particular man in a wheelchair purposely tried to run over my tools. I would push him away, and he would come straight back at my tools with his wheelchair. I had to do something. I found some huge stuffed dining room chairs and built a barricade all around me and my tools. The barricade worked! My tools were safe. My wife entered the room and was shocked at the blockade she witnessed. What a circus, but the piano DID get tuned.

God Himself has solved some of my piano tuning complications. It's not unusual to encounter a barking dog when entering someone's home, but in one particular case, as I was tuning a piano, and after the dog had calmed down, I was informed that the residents had to leave. They assured me that their dog would not bark and left me and the dog to tune the piano. However, as soon as they were out of the driveway, the dog started up. His barking was so severe there was no way I could hear the beats to tune. I wondered what to do, and then I prayed. I turned to the dog and sternly commanded it to shut up in the name of Jesus Christ. The dog did not make one more peep until I finished the tuning. I grabbed my tools to leave, and as soon as I took one step out the door, the dog began barking again.

Here's some more humor from my piano technician career. I entered a home to tune a small upright piano. The lady who greeted me at the door was very sweet and gracious. She showed me the piano and left the room. Her little girl came in to watch me. When I started checking out the piano, I was horrified at what I heard. Never before had I ever encountered a piano this out of whack. Believe it or not, the bass was sharper than the treble. The rest of the piano made no sense at all. Looking at the little girl, I jokingly said, "Did your mother try to tune this piano?" Her mother heard my question and ran into the room, her face beet red. She embarrassingly admitted she had tried. I was just as embarrassed as she was. But it all ended well. The piano sounded great; it just took a long time to tune.

Kids are funny and cute. Several times I've had the door opened to find a young child running to his mom to announce that the "tune man is here." I think that's a fun title; don't you?

One time a customer asked me why they didn't tune the strings before they put them into the piano. He was dead serious. I could have made a snappy, sarcastic comment, but that would not have promoted my business. So I nicely and calmly answered his question.

Then there was the singing basset hound. He was an enthusiastic singer, but way off key. The owner solved the problem by putting him in the basement.

Have you ever heard the phrase, "I'll get your goat"? Well, listen to this. A few years ago I was driving up to a customer's home out in the country and encountered a couple of goats. One goat was much bigger than the other, and both of them seemed friendly and overly curious. When I opened the car door the big goat began to climb in. Before I realized what was happening he was halfway into the front seat. The only way I could remove him was to grab him by the neck and pull him back across my lap so I could push him out of the car. That took most of my strength, and I'm not a weak person. I got my tools, walked up to the front door, and was ushered in by a very nice lady who showed me to the piano. A very friendly dog walked up to me, and I petted him for a minute. Then I noticed a cat lying on the couch. In this friendly atmosphere, I made the mistake of assuming the cat was also friendly. When I reached to pet her I was rewarded with a blood-curdling war cry and barely removed my tuning hand in time to prevent getting it clawed by the cat. At that point, the lady's son entered the room and told me the cat was possessed. Needless to say, I stayed clear of that cat for the duration of my stay.

Oh the hazards of being a piano technician!!! Despite these instances, I've had thousands of wonderful encounters with people over the forty years that I've been tuning. I love my career, and I'm grateful for the many divine appointments I've experienced over the decades.

16

WHAT IS A FALSE PROPHET?

*Beware of false prophets, which come to you in sheep's
clothing, but inwardly they are ravening wolves.
Ye shall know them by their fruits.*

MATTHEW 7:15,16A

There are a couple of men I really respect as prophets who were wrong about their predictions in the 2020 U.S. presidential election. Immediately, after the election, many people labeled them as false prophets. Are they really false prophets? Does an erroneous prediction make one a false prophet?

> *But the prophet, which shall presume to speak a word in my name, which I have not commanded him to speak, or that shall speak in the name of other gods, even that prophet shall die.*
>
> *And if thou say in thine heart, How shall we know the word which the LORD hath not spoken?*

When a prophet speaketh in the name of the LORD, if the thing follow not, nor come to pass, that is the thing which the LORD hath not spoken, but the prophet hath spoken it presumptuously: thou shalt not be afraid of him.

Deuteronomy 18:20-22

According to these verses, a prophet who prophesied something in the name of the Lord that didn't come to pass should die. But that was the old covenant. We have a new covenant today with far more grace and mercy than the Old Testament. But has the way God looks at a prophet changed?

I'm glad I'm not a prophet in the Old Testament. That would have been a lot of pressure. If you study the purpose of prophets in the Old Testament, you see how critical it was that the prophet got things right. Only a very few people in the Old Testament had the Holy Spirit, and it was conditional. They could lose it, and some did. The directives from God for Israel were generally delivered to the king via a prophet. Israel's well-being depended upon the accuracy of his words.

In the New Testament everyone who is born again has the Holy Spirit as a permanent gift. We can all hear from God directly. We all have the responsibility to hear from God individually and direct our lives accordingly. Also, the emphasis of prophecy has switched from being directive (Old Testament) to edification, exhortation, and comfort (New Testament). This does not exclude the possibility of prophecy being directive today.

But he that prophesieth speaketh unto men to edifi-
cation, and exhortation, and comfort.

1 Corinthians 14:3

Another thing to consider is that most prophecies given with future fulfillment today are conditional. In order to see the good things carried out by God, it's required to cooperate with Him. There was a prophetic word once given to a friend of mine that he would make a lot of money with a particular business. But he never took any steps to initiate the business, and decided he'd been given a false word when it didn't happen. The truth is that he never did anything to allow the fulfillment of his prophetic word. How can God bless and prosper a business that doesn't even exist?

According to Matthew 7:15, 16a (our theme Scripture for this chapter), a false prophet looks good on the outside, but he is evil on the inside. The fruit they bring forth in their life is rotten.

But there were false prophets also among the people, even as there shall be false teachers among you, who privily shall bring in damnable heresies, even de-nying the Lord that bought them, and bring upon themselves swift destruction.

And many shall follow their pernicious ways; by rea-son of whom the way of truth shall be evil spoken of.

And through covetousness shall they with feigned words make merchandise of you: whose judgment now of a long time lingereth not, and their damnation slumbereth not.

2 Peter 2:1-3

False prophets are likened to false teachers who use people for their own gain.

False prophets lead people away from the true God to worship other things. The tendency is that people who listen to false prophets are also drawn to the prophet as an object of worship.

The true test of a prophet is to look at the fruit of his ministry. The two men I mentioned at the beginning of this article are currently leading people to God and their followers are growing in godly understanding. Just because their predictions were wrong does not make them a false prophet from God's New Testament standard.

Some well-known ministers I've personally seen bring more attention to how great they are as opposed to how great God is. This is another example of steering people away from God. In fact, you can use this yourself as a litmus test when listening to preachers.

Be very careful about speaking evil about God's ministers. Freely throwing out accusations about one person or another being a false prophet is at best very unwise. Note that King Saul tried to kill David for many years, yet David never spoke evil of him because he knew God had anointed Saul to be king.

If a minister is off the ball, our heart should be to restore him, but we don't want to encourage others to listen to false words.

A false prophet is someone who looks good on the outside, but has evil motives on the inside. Most likely their information is coming from demons. The fruit of their ministry will be bad, and they will tend to lead people away from God.

There are many good prophets in the body of Christ today. Let's embrace the hope they bring. We must have hope to stay afloat in the times we live.

17

YOU CAN'T WIN USING THE DEVIL'S TACTICS

By this shall all men know that ye are my disciples, if ye have love one to another.

JOHN 13:35

When listening to politicians speak, most of the time it seems to me that rather than proclaiming how to fix our country's problems, they talk like fifth graders having an argument. They use name-calling, lies, deceit, etc. It happens on both sides.

I have been appalled that many times politically-minded people who claim to be Christians use the same tactics that the ungodly politicians use to get political advantage over their opponents. They use lying, bad-mouthing, gossip, etc. They even use these tactics against others who claim to be conservative Christians.

There's a song that goes like this: "They'll know we're Christians by our love." That needs to become a reality if we're going to make a positive impact in our world. Jesus taught us even to love our enemies. Saying we're Christians and acting like hypocrites gives God a bad name.

Another example of Christians falling into the devil's tactics is in internet marketing. We have learned that many so-called Christians use false urgency, exaggerations, and withholding truth to promote their products. People often give in to the enemy's methods, thinking that it's the normal way of doing business. I'm not saying all Christians do that, but it is a common practice. If people promote their products in a dignified, loving, and godly manner, and stand up for what's right, then they are positioning themselves for God's favorable intervention. This does not exclude shrewdness in a godly way.

We can't expect to use the devil's tactics and win. First of all, God won't back us. Secondly, Satan is far too clever to let us get ahead using his methods. The only way we can win is to fight God's way and have Him promote us. We must walk in love, especially with other Christians.

If we do things God's way, He will promote us and cause us to prosper. We may go through some hard times, but in the end, we'll come out ahead.

Anyone who genuinely tries to walk in love and godly standards in our day and time will certainly stand out. The darker things get, the brighter the light appears. Let's do our best to walk in love, and keep God's standards: honesty, clarity, service, and kindness to name a few. If we do, although we'll get resistance, we'll make a positive impact on this world and help to change the tide.

18

ARE YOU A SINNER SAVED BY GRACE?

Nay, in all these things we are more than conquerors through him that loved us.

ROMANS 8:37

What does the Bible say? Absolutely, we are saved by grace (Ephesians 2:8). There's nothing we can do in our own strength to be saved. You can't be good enough to earn salvation; it has to be by grace. We would be doomed to eternal death if it weren't for the grace of God. Once we accept Christ as the savior we are sons. Our identity changes. We no longer are sinners saved by grace; we have graduated to sonship with our heavenly Father.

> *Beloved, now are we the sons of God, and it doth not yet appear what we shall be: but we know that, when he shall appear, we shall be like him; for we shall see him as he is.*
>
> 1 John 3:2

According to Romans 3:22, we have the righteousness of God. If we stay in the mentality of being sinners, we will never bring forth the abundance of good fruit God has put in our path. Although we are legally righteous sons of God, we will be inhibited from manifesting His righteousness. The devil will more likely be able to beat us down with condemnation, guilt, fear, and other such negativity.

With a mindset of being a sinner who happens to be saved by grace, instead of the elevated approach of identifying as a child of God, we will probably lead a defensive life instead of remaining on the offense as more than a conqueror (Romans 8:37).

Certainly, if we sin, we should immediately run to God, confess it, and get over it. Our mindset needs to be focused on our righteousness as a son, not on our sin.

A wonderful Christian minister whom I've listened to for years has the following to say about when God looks at you with your problems. He doesn't see what's wrong with you; He sees what's missing in your relationship with Him, and that's the point of your next miracle. This is a brilliant way to approach our issues. It really helps one to stay positive.

It's one thing to be actively engaged in willful sin, but for us who really want to live for God, we need to be righteousness-minded. God's mercies never end; He's always there to help us.

We are no longer sinners saved by grace. We are righteous sons saved by grace. Instead of thinking of yourself as a sinner who sometimes gets it right, think of yourself as a saint who sometimes misses it. You'll have a much more joyful and powerful walk with the Lord if you do. The fruit you bring forth and your life in general will be much greater.

Here are some other points to consider. God knows we're going to sin and make mistakes. God is most concerned that we get back on track with Him. He's not a human that holds onto sin-consciousness and guilt; nor is He out to punish us. He wants us to get on with it and get back to His program.

Don't let mistakes hold you back. How can you walk with God while you are holding on to junk that is contrary to Him? Let it go, and receive His forgiveness and peace.

Don't forget your life is not your own. I've witnessed some who are so guilt-conscious that they quit. Some have gone to the extreme of ending their own life. How tragic. They were bought with a price; it wasn't their life to take. God has blessings for each of us to utilize so that we can reach others for Him. If you get knocked down, confess your sins and get back into the fight. There's nothing God can't fix.

> *For a just man falleth seven times, and riseth up again...*
>
> Proverbs 24:16

God even takes the bad and turns it into good.

> *And we know that all things work together for good to them that love God, to them who are the called according to his purpose.*

Romans 8:28

You are God's anointed. Let's manifest God's power and flourish. Let Him show His love through you.

19

DO I HAVE TO GO TO CHURCH TO BE A CHRISTIAN?

Not forsaking the assembling of ourselves together, as the manner of some is; but exhorting one another: and so much the more, as ye see the day approaching.

HEBREWS 10:25

I meet with all kinds of people in my piano tuning business. I love my work; I love people; and I love sharing the Gospel with them. I get to share just about every day.

Many times I meet people who say they are Christian, but they don't go to church. It's usually because they got hurt by people in the church who were either acting ignorantly or hypocritically. Unfortunately, there is a lot of hypocrisy and ignorance among churchgoers.

I believe the basis for becoming a Christian is Romans 10:9, 10. According to those verses when you confess Jesus as Lord and believe in your heart that God has raised him from the dead, you are saved, that is, born again. Hence you are a Christian. Christ lives in you via the Holy Spirit.

However, that's just the start. We also need other more mature Christians to help us change our lives and live the new life available through Jesus.

Christianity was not meant to be a lone ranger experience. We are united in one body, and we need each other. Ephesians 4:15, 16 says that the whole body grows and compacts together as we interact.

The devil and his cohorts love to isolate Christians. They are then easily picked off. We don't want to let him do that. The theme Scriptures says not to forsake the assembling of ourselves together.

Even though some churches abound in hypocrisy and compromise, not all do. We will never find a perfect church. The only perfect person that ever lived was Jesus himself, so we can't expect any man-made group to be perfect.

As we approach the end of this age, things will get worse and worse in the world. We'll need each other more and more.

I tell people who don't want to go to church to at least find a group of strong Christians with whom to fellowship together regularly. If we use the excuse that we were hurt so we don't fellowship with other Christians, I doubt that will fly when we stand before Jesus for judgment.

The proper thing to do is forgive where we've been hurt and find a group we can meld with. Let's fellowship with other like-minded believers and get stronger.

20

YOU ARE CALLED TO FULL-TIME MINISTRY

Now then we are ambassadors for Christ, as though God did beseech you by us: we pray you in Christ's stead, be ye reconciled to God.

2 CORINTHIANS 5:20

When you become a Christian, you are an ambassador for Christ. An ambassador is one who represents his nation to a foreign nation. Whether we like it or not, we are ambassadors for Christ, ambassadors from the Kingdom of Heaven to the earth. We determine whether we will be good ones or bad ones. God has given us the Word of Reconciliation to accomplish our task.

God has placed us in the body of Christ as it has pleased Him. As we continue to serve Him, our particular calling will become clearer and clearer.

For we are his workmanship, created in Christ Jesus unto good works, which God hath before ordained that we should walk in them.

Ephesians 2:10

God has specific good works for each one of us for which we were ordained a long time ago.

What do you like to do? Generally, that's where God has gifted you. My wife is a very good organizer and administrator; I am not. I am good at music and teaching. I would make a horrible bank teller or accountant, but I am a very good piano tuner. Let's run in our own lane and not envy someone else's gifting.

There are the five-fold ministry gifts listed in Ephesians 5:11. They are apostles, prophets, evangelists, pastors, and teachers. Not everyone has these gifts. The gifts are not to the individuals that carry them, but rather, their lives are a gift to the church. The purpose of the five-fold ministry gifts is not to do the work of the ministry, but to train the people to do the work.

Many times in our culture, church is like an entertainment show. The pastor performs, and the people sit in the pews and enjoy his presentation. It's like going to a movie. The people think that if they go to church, they've done their job as a Christian. The pastor is a paid entertainer. That's not the way it should be.

A pastor is one of the five-fold ministry gifts. In our culture, pastor is the term given to the paid position of the man leading the church. Biblically, this is not necessarily so. The head leader of a church doesn't necessarily have to be a pastor, and if you are a pastor, it doesn't mean you are the head of a church. I have had it prophesied over me that I'm a pastor. I've never led a church, nor have I had the desire to do so, but I have ministered and counseled as a pastor for years. I've even pastored others thousands of miles away over the phone.

If you do have a five-fold ministry gift, it is not a title. It is a function; it is not anything to flaunt. A person who has a gift of administration, mercy, or hospitality is just as valuable to God as an evangelist.

We all have gifts and callings of God. In reality, we are all called to full-time ministry, no matter how we function. I use my piano tuning business just about every day as a platform for evangelism and ministry. I've seen countless people get touched by prophetic words I give and the Bible I share. I love it.

As a pastor friend of mine said, "Just show up for work, and God will give you something to do." Showing up for work means to have a willing heart to serve.

We all have a sphere of influence. Don't underestimate your calling. Someone had to lead Billy Graham to the Lord, and he in turn led millions. If you are called to full-time, paid ministry, great. If not, you are no less valuable. As the saying goes, "Bloom where you are planted."

21

THE GREATEST EVENT
OF ALL HISTORY

E xtra! Extra! Grab your free tickets!

The greatest event of all history is about to take place. Don't miss out. Get your ticket now! Tickets are FREE. It's the great event. It's gonna take place shortly! Get your ticket now before it's too late. It's already been paid for. All you need to do is receive one. And you will be taking part in the greatest drama known to man, a play with one act.

Romans 10:9, 10 tells you how. You'll find the details of admittance in those two verses. If you miss out on this play, you'll really be sorry. If you don't get your ticket in time, you'll be forced to pay for a ticket to the next event afterward, and you will be forced to attend. This second play will be horribly depressing and wrought with terror. You probably won't get out of it alive. That's a hell of a way to go.

So don't miss out on this upcoming greatest event. You can get better seats if you are willing to pay a price. Live according to God's Word and you'll earn upgrades. Box seats are available if you qualify for crowns. The food will be scrumptious; the music divine; the joyful atmosphere will last for eternity; and sadness will be gone.

Don't worry about losing your ticket once you've acquired it. It will be engraved on your heart.

What is this event? It's called the rapture of the church. It's free to all. There are plenty of seats for everybody. Get your ticket now and pursue upgrades. Time is running out. Don't miss it. It will be the time of your life.

22

WILL CHRISTIANS LIVE ETERNALLY IN HEAVEN?

*For this we say unto you by the word of the Lord, that
we which are alive and remain unto the coming of the
Lord shall not prevent them which are asleep.
For the Lord himself shall descend from heaven with
a shout, with the voice of the archangel, and with the
trump of God: and the dead in Christ shall rise first:
Then we which are alive and remain shall be caught
up together with them in the clouds, to meet the Lord
in the air: and so shall we ever be with the Lord.*

1 THESSALONIANS 4:15-17

I believe most Christians think that going to heaven is their biggest goal, and that once they get there, they will be there for eternity in bliss. Let's see what the Scriptures have to say about this.

Many Christians spend their whole life working and hoping they'll make it to heaven.

For by grace are ye saved through faith; and that not of yourselves: it is the gift of God.

Ephesians 2:8

According to this verse, we are saved by grace. It's not dependent on whether we're good or bad. Eternal life with God is dependent only on accepting Jesus Christ as our Savior.

That if thou shalt confess with thy mouth the Lord Jesus, and shalt believe in thine heart that God hath raised him from the dead, thou shalt be saved.

For with the heart man believeth unto righteousness; and with the mouth confession is made unto salvation.

Romans 10:9, 10

However, living for God after we're saved is important. It will determine our quality of life now as well as our eternal rewards after we meet the Lord in the air.

Every man's work shall be made manifest: for the day shall declare it, because it shall be revealed by fire; and the fire shall try every man's work of what sort it is.

If any man's work abide which he hath built thereupon, he shall receive a reward.

If any man's work shall be burned, he shall suffer loss: but he himself shall be saved; yet so as by fire.

1 Corinthians 3:13-15

According to the theme Scripture, we will be with the Lord forever. Where will the Lord be? He will be in heaven for a while after the rapture, which is when we meet the Lord in the air. But we don't know how long that will last. As presented in Revelation 20, Jesus will return to earth and destroy the antichrist and his kingdom, and He will reign over the entire world. We will be coming back with Him.

After He comes back, He will set up what people call the millennial kingdom and reign for 1000 years. At that point, we will be with Him on earth.

> *And he laid hold on the dragon, that old serpent, which is the Devil, and Satan, and bound him a thousand years,*
>
> *And cast him into the bottomless pit, and shut him up, and set a seal upon him, that he should deceive the nations no more, till the thousand years should be fulfilled: and after that he must be loosed a little season.*
>
> Revelation 20:2, 3

Depending on how we live now will determine what position we will have with Him. But this is not the end.

After the thousand years, and the great white throne judgment of Revelation 20:11, there will come a new heaven and new earth.

Jesus will reign forever, but not in heaven. He will rule from the New Jerusalem which will be on a new earth. Where will we be? Again, we'll be on earth, not in heaven.

Jesus referred to Paradise when speaking to the repentant criminal on the cross next to Him. Paradise is on earth, not in heaven. Paradise is heaven on earth. As human beings, we are earth dwellers. Angels live in heaven.

Sorry to shatter your illusion of being in heaven forever, but I'm sure we'll really enjoy eternal paradise here on earth. We won't be disappointed.

23

WHAT WILL IT BE LIKE IN OUR NEW BODY?

*Who shall change our vile body, that it may be fashioned
like unto his glorious body, according to the working
whereby he is able even to subdue all things unto himself.*

PHILIPPIANS 3:21

In my teenage years, as I recall, guys would look at girls and rate their looks on a scale from one to ten. We were far more interested in looks than what their character was like. I think in a lot of ways, we were pretty mean. But that's past, and in my case, it's been confessed as a sin and forgiven.

The theme verse of this chapter, Philippians 3:21, says that our present body will be changed to be like Christ's glorious body at His resurrection. In 1 Corinthians 15, it says we will get a spiritual body instead of the natural body we have today.

It is sown a natural body; it is raised a spiritual body. There is a natural body, and there is a spiritual body.

1 Corinthians 15:44

I'm sure that our future spiritual bodies would be rated ten by my past teenage standards. We will no longer be subject to death and sickness. Nor will we be bothered by fears and insecurities. These things will be in the past.

Just for fun, let's explore what we can look forward to in our future spiritual body. Whatever Christ could do in His resurrected body, we will also be able to do in our future spiritual bodies.

In John 20:26, Jesus appeared to His disciples behind closed doors. He didn't knock or break the door down. Somehow He appeared in a locked room without opening any doors. Maybe we'll be able to walk through walls. When the men on the road to Emmaus recognized Him at dinner, He disappeared. When Mary saw Jesus at the tomb, she didn't recognize Him. Apparently, He could change His appearance.

One of the first things Jesus did after His resurrection is recorded in 1 Peter 3:19. Jesus went and preached, or actually proclaimed His victory, to demons who were responsible for corrupting the world in Noah's day. They are being held in a spiritual prison until future judgments. Jesus could travel from the natural realm to the spiritual realm. In the natural realm, He still ate food, as mentioned in John 21:13. Jesus knew people, and remembered former things that happened.

> *And so it is written, The first man Adam was made a living soul; the last Adam was made a quickening spirit.*
>
> 1 Corinthians 15:45

In our present bodies, we are empowered by soul life. We all know our souls sometimes get weary. When we get our spiritual bodies, we will be empowered by a quickening (Old English for life-giving) spirit.

Think of yourself without any emotional or physical problems. What could you accomplish? Life would always be joyful and restful. We'll have work to do, but it will be enjoyable and fulfilling. We will have a great eternity.

I'll gladly trade this body for a glorified body. We absolutely will get one at the rapture. In the meantime, we should live for God the best we can and take care of what we have. A glorious future awaits us.

24

KILL THE VICTIM BEFORE
THE VICTIM KILLS YOU

*For whatsoever is born of God overcometh the world: and
this is the victory that overcometh the world, even our faith.*

1 JOHN 5:4

My mother was one of five girls. Most of her life she had severe problems with depression. She spent most of her savings on psychiatrists and psycho-therapy. One of my earliest memories of her is when she went into the hospital for shock treatments. I was around three years old, and I didn't think I'd ever see her again.

All through her life, she told everybody how bad her growing-up experience was. She spoke of her sisters picking on her constantly, especially one in particular. She was always trying to get people to feel sorry for her.

I had very similar problems. I was constantly depressed, had digestive problems due to stress, and was often telling people how traumatic my childhood was. I was very similar to my mother, although I didn't do any of the medical stuff she did. I did, though, see a social worker for a while after my parents divorced. I was around twelve years old when they split up..

I remember complaining to my aunt Marilyn, my mother's youngest sister, with whom I was very close, how bad it was growing up with my mother. She said I had a right to feel the way I did. At that moment, a light went off in my brain. This is what I thought: "So what if I'm justified in the way I feel? I'm miserable and sick. If I keep thinking this way, I'm trapped. I want to get out of this trap. I don't want to stay here."

Probably within five years of that incident I became a Christian. The group I was involved with had much instruction about renewed mind as well as positive thinking and confessions. I saw a possibility of freedom. I started practicing some of the things I was learning, and started to see some change. I did student teaching during my last quarter of college, and I am convinced that if I hadn't become a Christian and started practicing some of the things I was learning, I never would have had the confidence to do my student teaching. Although I never pursued a career in math teaching, I did quite well in my student teaching.

Growing up, I had a victim mentality which I learned from my mother who also had a victim mentality. I hold no grudges against her. She kept a job, food on the table, and a roof over our heads. That's about all she could do. I'm happy to report that she got saved before the end of her life.

I remember hearing a testimony from Joyce Meyer, a well-known Bible teacher whom I highly respect. She came from a very abusive background. She complained about her upbringing, and God said to her, "Do you want to be pitiful or powerful?" She couldn't be both. She decided she wanted to be powerful, and with God's help overcame her past. She has had a worldwide influence with her ministry. I want to be powerful, don't you?

You can't always control your circumstances, but you can control how you react to them. If someone or something else is responsible for the way you feel, there would be no hope for you unless the other one changes. However, that's not the case.

Although for a while, people might come and try to console and help you in your pity parties, they won't stick around forever. My mother's sisters, as well as many others, eventually got sick of her complaining. The only ones who will stick around the pity party forever are Satan's demons. They'll make you and everybody else miserable. As bad as your story is, there's always someone who had it worse.

We should be compassionate with people and try to help them. But we don't want to enable people to stay in their misery. If people want to stay miserable and refuse help, perhaps we should move on to someone who wants help. With God's help we can change the way we think, and God can use our bad past to help others.

And we know that all things work together for good to them that love God, to them who are the called according to his purpose.

Romans 8:28

In our society today the victim mentality is celebrated.

Don't stay a victim. It's a dead end. We're more than conquerors through Jesus Christ.

Nay, in all these things we are more than conquerors through him that loved us.

Romans 8:37

Kill the victim before the victim kills you.

25

HOW TO TREAT A SICK PERSON

Beloved, I wish above all things that thou mayest prosper
and be in health, even as thy soul prospereth.

3 JOHN 2

A friend of mine who is a Bible teacher, recently shared about his prior experiences in the Word of Faith movement. I was shocked. He said that if someone who was sick didn't get healed supernaturally by God, others in the movement would judge him and condemn him for not having enough faith to get healed. Certainly, this would cause him to feel worse.

A number of years ago, I heard the following story from an older gentleman named Paul who had been a leader in a Christian movement. He had had a heart attack, and needed some major medical attention to save his life. A younger man, sitting under his tutelage, said to Paul, "I can no longer follow your leadership since you don't have enough faith to get healed." How can anyone be that insensitive? Paul was a wonderful, compassionate man who loved God and people.

In my Christian upbringing, I was taught that the medical field was third aid instead of first aid. First aid was going to God yourself; second aid was getting another believer to pray with you. Third aid was the medical profession. I like that model. It has saved me a lot of time and money.

One of my pastors said when someone is sick, they don't need to be judged or told they don't have enough faith. They need love. How true that is. I know from personal experience how hard it is to "muster up enough faith" to get healed. Why add insult to injury when someone already feels bad?

It's not a sin to go to a doctor. The problem comes when someone makes the medical field God. I had a customer once who was a wonderful Christian lady who was sick all the time. Every time I was around her, she was telling me what the latest doctor said. I believe she'd have been a lot better off taking a stand for God, and not putting her trust so much in the medical field. But I was always kind to her, and prayed for her many times.

God can, and many times, does lead people to doctors. Here's the story of another friend of mine. He was suddenly struck very ill when he was out of town teaching a three-day presentation. He didn't know what was wrong with him, but after those three days, God literally told him to go to the emergency room. He arrived to discover his appendix had burst and was rushed into surgery. Supernatural healing and medical treatment are not mutually exclusive. They were dumbfounded that he managed to stay alive those three previous days. But he was functioning according to the leading of Holy Spirit. He said he slept most of the time, waking only when it was time to teach.

Another friend named Carl was the leader of a ministry that made missionary trips to Romania to minister mostly to Gypsies. He told me of the many healing miracles that occurred. He himself had been supernaturally healed of a broken neck, a broken wrist, and many other things. He said that God allowed doctors because of our unbelief.

It is true in many instances that people don't have enough faith to get healed supernaturally by God. But the truth is that God wants you well. Note our theme Scripture above: 3 John 2. God wants you well. Sickness doesn't glorify God.

God can use sickness to bring about humility and other lessons to us, but HE DOESN'T CAUSE THE SICKNESS. He turns lemons into lemonade.

When someone is sick, let's show compassion. Be sure to pray for them. If they want to go to a doctor, that's their individual choice; there's no condemnation.

26

GOD WANTS YOU HEALED NOW

*Who his own self bare our sins in his own body on
the tree, that we, being dead to sins, should live unto
righteousness: by whose stripes ye were healed.*

1 PETER 2:24

There are many opinions and doctrines about God's supernatural healing. Some say it doesn't take place today. Some say it only happens if it's God's will. Some say you have to be living a good life to get healed. I'm sure there are many other opinions.

Jesus Christ is supposed to be our example. What took place in His ministry? Jesus healed everyone he touched. Only one time is it recorded that he prayed more than once to get complete results. It does say He didn't see a lot of miracles in His hometown. But it wasn't because when He prayed for people it didn't work. People from His hometown didn't approach Him in mass numbers because they didn't believe in Him. They were too familiar with Him.

As far as healing and deliverance for people He ministered to, Jesus had a 100% success rate. He never said, "God is using this sickness to make you a better person." Nor did He say, "God allowed this because He loves you," or, "Come back in a year; it's not God's timing." Jesus never used these cliches we often hear in our faith communities.

Jesus is our standard. In Mark 9 we see the example where a father brought his demonized son to Jesus' disciples, and they couldn't heal him. Jesus came and solved the problem. He said to the father, "If thou canst believe, all things are possible to him that believeth." The father said, "Lord, I believe; help thou mine unbelief." Then Jesus freed the boy. Later, Jesus told the disciples they couldn't heal the boy because of their unbelief. Never does it say that God didn't want to heal the boy.

The father recognized his unbelief and prayed for that to be adjusted. Later Jesus told His disciples that THEIR unbelief hindered the success.

> *Then came the disciples to Jesus apart, and said, Why could not we cast him out?*
>
> *And Jesus said unto them, Because of your unbelief: for verily I say unto you, If ye have faith as a grain of mustard seed, ye shall say unto this mountain, Remove hence to yonder place; and it shall remove; and nothing shall be impossible unto you.*
>
> Matthew 17:19, 20

Notice that after Jesus told them their lack of results was due to their unbelief, He also explained what faith can do. He told them with faith, they could move mountains.

We need faith to heal others, whether they believe or not. Our faith grows as we reach out and pray. You might say you've never seen anyone get out of a wheelchair, but I will counter that with, "How many in wheelchairs have you prayed for?" Your faith will grow as you boldly step out and pray for the sick.

In my experience today, I also don't always see success. But I don't blame the sick person, and say that their lack of faith was the problem. I simply continue praying for others, and the more people I pray for, the more successes I see. My own faith is continually growing as I see Jesus bringing the needed deliverance.

I have seen many people healed supernaturally by God for whom I've prayed. But certainly not all. I know from my personal experience that bitterness and unforgiveness can make a person sick. There are a lot of other things that can open the door to sickness and bondage also. We don't yet have the perfectly renewed mind of Christ. However, as we continue to serve God, our faith grows and we will see more results.

I've seen some people for whom I've prayed getting healed over a period of time. Many people were instantaneously healed, and stayed healed. Some were healed and later lost their healing. Why all these scenarios? I don't know. One thing I do know is that if I had never stepped out and prayed, nothing would have happened. Even if nothing changed, people were still thankful that I cared enough to pray.

Jesus had a 100% success rate. That's our standard. Don't lower the standard because it's not your experience. There's no condemnation. Just keep on praying for people, and the results will get better.

God wants you healed now. Let's keep that as the standard. Keep in the fight, and results will continue to improve more and more.

27

WHAT DO YOU THINK ABOUT GOD?

Or despisest thou the riches of his goodness and forbearance and longsuffering; not knowing that the goodness of God leadeth thee to repentance?

ROMANS 2:4

I recently watched a video where there was a correlation made between attitude towards God and T-cells in the blood, which affect the immune system. The more T-cells, the better. Three groups of people were studied, two of them Christian. One group was Christians who thought of God as a cruel taskmaster waiting to beat them down and judge them for their sins. The second group was atheists. The third group was composed of Christians who thought of God as a loving, benevolent Father, there to nurture them, encourage them, and take care of them. The results were somewhat surprising. The most unhealthy were the Christians who thought of God as a mean, hard taskmaster. The next group in the middle was the atheists. The most healthy group was the Christians who thought of God as a good Father.

Mary and I know the daughter of old friends of ours who turned to witchcraft and rejected Christ. She was raised in a Christian environment, but she reasoned that the Christian God was an angry God. I used to work with a man from a strong religious Christian background who thought that if we perhaps worked hard enough and behaved well enough, we might make it into heaven. Salvation is not determined by works.

> *For by grace are ye saved through faith; and that not of yourselves: it is the gift of God:*
>
> *Not of works, lest any man should boast.*
>
> Ephesians 2:8, 9

Mary and I once attended a church where the pastor taught that more people hadn't received the baptism of the Holy Spirit because we were leading sinful lives, and the Holy Spirit wouldn't dwell in an unclean vessel. In other words, we had to clean up our lives first by our own efforts, and then the Holy Spirit would come in. I thought, "If that's the case, it's hopeless for me." In myself, I have no power to clean myself up. I need the Holy Spirit's power to clean up my act in the first place. The truth of the matter is that we don't get the Holy Spirit as a reward for being good; we get Him as a gift because we are so bad that we need Him. We are hopelessly lost without Him.

Mary once led a girl into the baptism of the Holy Spirit who was gay, an alcoholic, a drug addict, and ran a ring of prostitutes. She, at the time, was high on crack. Mary explained the mechanics of speaking in tongues to her while she was experiencing this co-caine high. She tried it out, and it worked. She genuinely spoke in tongues. She herself was shocked. What really shocked her was that she immediately sobered up, and she stood in utter awe of the power of God. She exclaimed that anyone who does crack knows that one does not come down from a high like that. She avoided all the panic and sickness symptoms.

The Bible claims over and over that God is love. 1 Corinthians 13 describes in detail what God's love is like. It's long-suffering, kind, positive, compassionate, etc. The nine fruits of the spirit in Galatians 5:22 also show what God is like. They are "love, joy, peace, longsuffering, gentleness, goodness, faith, meekness, (and) temperance."

Religion and godliness are really two completely different concepts. Religion deals with behavior modification which tries to bring forth good spiritual fruit through fear, guilt, condemnation, and other negative motivations. It works from the outside in. This won't produce the results you want. Godliness, on the other hand, deals from the inside out. If our heart is changed, we will automatically bring forth the good fruit.

It's true that if we willfully defy God we will eventually receive judgment. But God is very long-suffering, kind, compassionate, and good. You may say, "Well, if God is so good, why is the world so unfair and evil?" A well-known Bible teacher answers this claim by saying, "If God weren't good, why did He send His son to die for us?"

God is infinitely good. He loves us. He's there to help us and never leaves us. What you think of God is the most important thing there is to determine the quality of your life.

28

HOW DO I SPEND TIME WITH GOD?

But seek ye first the kingdom of God, and his righteousness;
and all these things shall be added unto you.

MATTHEW 6:33

God is an invisible Spirit. I've wondered many times what is an effective way to spend time with Him. I've heard many opinions about it. Some say to get on your knees. Some say to just isolate yourself in your prayer closet for hours, and He'll show up. I've tried that, and I always go to sleep or get bored.

Psalms 100:4 says to enter His gates with thanksgiving, and His courts with praise. Some have made a law out of that, implying that God won't hear you without thanksgiving and praise. Read Psalms. Many times a psalm begins with a complaint about evil circumstances. That certainly is not thanksgiving or praise. David and other psalmists were genuine with God about how they felt. I'm sure God heard their cries.

On the other hand, let's not belittle thanksgiving and praise. They are very effective in ushering us into God's presence. That is guaranteed, but you don't prevent God from reaching you when you're not giving thanks or praise. The psalms show us how God involved Himself with David's and others' lives when they acknowledged God inside or outside of thanksgiving and praise.

The problem comes when people make their own rules and laws about anything, and spending time with God is no exception. They often determine the way for everyone by their own experiences. Be careful not to make a doctrine out of your experience.

I bet about every sincere Christian I know would say they don't spend enough time with God. How long should we spend? A half-hour a day? An hour? Two hours? I know this: we have to be intentional about spending time with God, or the enemy will make sure we don't. He'll make sure you are too busy.

What about fasting? Some insist that fasting helps you get close to God. Fasting with prayer is Biblical and a great way to seek God. Some, however, have problems fasting for medical reasons. Again, let's not make a law regarding this.

I believe God works with us individually. I am a musician, and I enjoy singing and playing gospel songs at the piano. These are musical get-togethers between God and me.

Many mornings I write a list of things I'm thankful for. God fills me with joy during this kind of exercise.

I try to read something from the Bible daily. I have found that reading God's Word out loud is very effective. I'm sure God listens when I'm reading.

Often, I'll write prophecies for myself or for things I'm concerned about. By prophecy, I mean writing inspired words from God. I believe I'm spending time with God right now as I write this chapter.

I've made resolutions many times about spending more time with God and doing things a certain way. I always fail to keep those resolutions going, and I end up in condemnation which I know is wrong. Of course, I also need to be on guard for laziness, as I know I can make excuses for not spending time with God.

This is not a one-size-fits-all activity. I believe God is pleased no matter what kind of effort you make to spend time with Him. He's not legalistic; we are. As you put forth effort, God will increase your enjoyment in spending time with Him. Rather than keeping it a discipline, it will become a delight.

Find out what works for you. God loves you, and He's your greatest fan. Seek Him, and you will find Him.

29

WHAT IS A PASTOR?

*And he gave some, apostles; and some, prophets; and
some, evangelists; and some, pastors and teachers;
For the perfecting of the saints, for the work of the
ministry, for the edifying of the body of Christ:*

EPHESIANS 4:11,12

In our culture a pastor is usually a paid position for the head leader of a congregation that meets in a certain building on a regular basis. Is that really what the Bible says a pastor is? As noted in Ephesians above, a pastor is one of the gifts to the body of believers, and it's a calling from the Lord Jesus Christ.

The Greek word for pastor in the above verse is *poimēn* which means *shepherd*, as well as *feeder*. A shepherd in Biblical days loved his sheep and would lay down his life for the sheep. He took care of the sheep and nurtured them. Matthew 18 and Luke 15 illustrate the extent of a true shepherd's care.

How think ye? if a man have an hundred sheep, and one of them be gone astray, doth he not leave the ninety and nine, and goeth into the mountains, and seeketh that which is gone astray?

Matthew 18:12

What man of you, having an hundred sheep, if he lose one of them, doth not leave the ninety and nine in the wilderness, and go after that which is lost, until he find it?

Luke 15:4

Graduating from a Bible college does not automatically make someone a pastor. Pastors are determined by Jesus Christ Himself. People are called to a pastorship by God. It is not something to be studied and learned; it is a calling from the Lord. The training at a Bible college could certainly make one a better pastor, but being educated into becoming a pastor is a false concept.

If you're called into one of the five-fold gift ministries, namely, an apostle, a prophet, a pastor, an evangelist, or a teacher, then you have that ministry for life. It is the Lord's calling. Note Romans 11.

For the gifts and calling of God are without repentance.

Romans 11:29

Even if you don't fulfill the calling, that does not strip away your purpose. In fact, Bible college is not necessary for fulfilling the function of being a pastor.

Dan Mohler, a wonderful well-known minister here in America, pastored a church for a number of years with fantastic results. He never attended any Bible college. He did, however, spend many hours fellowshipping with God in the Scriptures.

Another point is that a pastor may not be a head elder in a congregation. It was prophesied over me more than twenty years ago that I was a pastor. At first, I was horrified, because I did not want to lead a large denominational congregation. The person who gave me that prophecy then explained to me that I already was a pastor. I thought about my life and realized that I had been pastoring individuals for many years. I saw how my approach to people in tough situations brought a sense of comfort and hope to them. Also, I noted how they felt they could trust their hearts to me. My "congregation" consisted of friends, acquaintances, and even business-related persons on a phone line as far away as the opposite coast or even South Africa.

I have never been paid financially for operating in my calling. It simply comes naturally to me.

The gift ministries, including *pastor*, are not gifts to the individual who has the gift. His <u>life</u> is a gift to the Body of Christ at large. Although the person will have a long suit in the ministry to which he's called, the main purpose of the gift ministry is to mature the Body of Christ.

Another concept about the gift ministry is that the minister is supposed to train others to function the way he does. Prophets train people to prophesy. Evangelists train others to evangelize, and so forth.

Some people can have more than one of the five-fold gifts operating in them. Jesus operated all five. According to 1 Timothy, the Apostle Paul was not only an apostle, but also a teacher and a preacher. Preaching is normally in the category of evangelism.

> *Whereunto I am ordained a preacher, and an apostle, (I speak the truth in Christ, and lie not;) a teacher of the Gentiles in faith and verity.*
>
> 1 Timothy 2:7

I'm not advocating that we drastically alter the way the church operates in America, but we should understand things properly the way God set them up. He knows what He's doing.

30

SHOULD CHRISTIANS HAVE A LOT OF MONEY?

But thou shalt remember the LORD thy God: for it is he that giveth thee power to get wealth, that he may establish his covenant which he sware unto thy fathers, as it is this day.

DEUTERONOMY 8:18

In some Christian circles, and especially at certain times of the past, poverty was and is considered a virtue. The underlying theme was that things of the world were evil. Only spiritual things were good. Yet God says He wants us to prosper.

> *Bring ye all the tithes into the storehouse, that there may be meat in mine house, and prove me now herewith, saith the LORD of hosts, if I will not open you the windows of heaven, and pour you out a blessing, that there shall not be room enough to receive it.*
>
> Malachi 3:10

In the old covenant one of the blessings of tithing was material abundance. In the new covenant, we are not under a law to tithe, but God promises abundance if we share from our material goods with the right attitude.

> *But this I say, He which soweth sparingly shall reap also sparingly; and he which soweth bountifully shall reap also bountifully.*
>
> *Every man according as he purposeth in his heart, so let him give; not grudgingly, or of necessity: for God loveth a cheerful giver.*
>
> *And God is able to make all grace abound toward you; that ye, always having all sufficiency in all things, may abound to every good work:*
>
> 2 Corinthians 9:6-8

If we give bountifully, we will be blessed abundantly. In Deuteronomy 28, God expounds upon all the blessings His people will experience when they hearken to His words and ways. However, when they don't, they will fall under the curses listed in chapters 28 and 29. Poverty is one of those curses. He doesn't just tersely mention poverty either; He goes into extensive detail about how it will look. No rain for their crops, disease among their animals, foreigners pillaging and even invading their land. But all of this is under the topic of being cursed for not heeding His guidance.

Poverty is a curse, and Jesus Christ broke all curses against us.

> *Let him that stole steal no more: but rather let him*
> *labour, working with his hands the thing which is*
> *good, that he may have to give to him that needeth.*
>
> Ephesians 4:28

We should have enough to not only meet our own needs, but also enough to be able to bless others. The problem with having lots of money comes when people trust in their riches rather than God.

> *Charge them that are rich in this world, that they be*
> *not highminded, nor trust in uncertain riches, but*
> *in the living God, who giveth us richly all things to*
> *enjoy;*
>
> 1 Timothy 6:17

Material riches can be here today and gone tomorrow, but God is always here.

> *But they that will be rich fall into temptation and*
> *a snare, and into many foolish and hurtful lusts,*
> *which drown men in destruction and perdition.*
>
> 1 Timothy 6:9

If a person's motivation is to get rich, they open themselves to many temptations from the devil. The Bible has many warnings against trying to get rich.

For the love of money is a root of all kinds of evils. It is through this craving that some have wandered away from the faith and pierced themselves with many pangs.

1 Timothy 6:10 ESV

I think the English Standard Version has a more accurate translation of this verse than most versions. The love of money is the root of many evils, but not all evil. But notice, it's not money itself that is evil; it's the **love** of money that's evil. Money itself is just a tool. Money represents power to get things. Money can be used for good or evil.

Abraham, David, Solomon, and many others were made rich by God. But the temptation is to trust in wealth rather than God, and that gets you into big trouble. America has been a very wealthy country for two hundred years. Notice, however, that the government is legislating many ungodly policies. Apparently, the leaders' dependence is on wealth rather than God who generated the wealth in the first place.

Israel went into captivity many times because they trusted in other things than God. If they turned back to God, He always had a way to bring them back. We certainly need to turn back to God here as a nation.

Another point is that one can be very wealthy but live like a pauper. It's called a poverty mindset where he is afraid to spend money and enjoy it when he can. It's based on the fear that one needs to save everything he makes in case things go sour. In reality, God is always there to supply our needs no matter what's going on in the world.

I'm not saying we should waste our resources irresponsibly, but we don't need to hoard things for fear of the future.

In conclusion, money itself is not evil. The love of money is. If we are extremely rich financially, we have more resources to help others. Our focus should be on listening to God's guidance for how to spend it. Helping the body of Christ will trump self-indulgence. It's not wrong to be wealthy, but you'll have to deal with the temptation to trust in your riches and not in God. Also the more you have, the more responsibility you have.

On the other side of the coin (no pun intended), God calls poverty a curse. God always wants you to have your needs met, and to have extra to help others.

ABOUT THE AUTHOR

Ron lives with his wife Mary of thirty-eight years. Together they both enjoy music as well as book writing. They both have been Christians for fifty years, and they love to host home Bible fellowships.

Ron loves to teach Biblical concepts to gatherings in various venues including churches. He often enriches these meetings with his own music. If there's not a piano present, he can bring his guitar. He amazes individuals when he makes up a personal song for someone in the audience. In reality, this is prophetic singing, which he loves to do.

If you are interested in contacting him for either speaking or musical performance, you can reach him by email: RonGordon515@gmail.com. His wife generally accompanies him, and she joins his musical performance with flute or voice.

Ron has recorded three albums of original music. His wife's flute playing is also featured on each album. You can find his music on YouTube. You can find a link to his YouTube channel by opening www.solo.to/marygordon or scanning the QR code to the right.

Ron Gordon's YouTube Channel

By trade, Ron is a piano technician. He began his business, Gordon Piano Service, in 1988. Tuning pianos is not only a hobby for him, but it also provides an amazing platform for ministry. Whether he's at someone's home, a church, or even a school, he always carries on

Visit Gordon Piano Service

a personal conversation with his customers. This gives him great access to their hearts, and it allows him to share the Scriptures with them. Many of the experiences in this book are examples of times with customers.

A cute story he loves to tell is about when he first learned piano tuning. He needed a piano while learning his new skills. You might imagine the discord that would fill the air when someone is first learning to tune the piano. Ron was not yet married, and he lived in a young couple's home. They were only too glad when Ron finished the course and decided to sell the piano. He found a buyer named Mary who later became his wife. That's how he got his piano back. He often jokes that it was the most expensive piano he ever purchased.

Mary has written three books. Her first book, *Inspired Moments of Truth, A Book of Poetry* is a collection of rhythmic delights downloaded from God during her prayer times. Videos of her reading a sampling from her book are located at www.inspiredmomentsoftruth.com

Inspired Moments of Truth

Mary's second book, *Escaping Loneliness in Marriage, 5 Crucial Concepts to Feel Loved in a Volatile Marriage* was written when she realized the deliverance they enjoyed after trauma in their early years of marriage would help others. www.escapinglonelinessinmarriage.com

Escaping Loneliness in Marriage

Mary's third book, *Sky-Hitching to Heaven, Experiencing the Fun Side of God* is a collection of amazing experiences in her life where God showed up in fun and unique ways. Her topics vary from whitewater canoeing to sky-hitching from the Midwest to

Sky-Hitching to Heaven

Washington state to mentoring a crack addict who ran a ring of girls, to cooking escapades and even shopping.

Ron has a great passion for helping people find God and grow in their relationship with Him. He knows that the only solution to the world's problems is Jesus Christ.

www.ingramcontent.com/pod-product-compliance
Lightning Source LLC
Chambersburg PA
CBHW060536130626
46553CB00002B/782